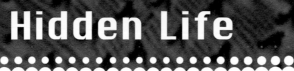

## Hidden Life

# What's Living in Your Classroom?

### Andrew Solway

**Heinemann**
LIBRARY

 **www.heinemann.co.uk/library**
Visit our website to find out more information about **Heinemann Library** books.

To order:
 Phone 44 (0) 1865 888066
Send a fax to 44 (0) 1865 314091
 Visit the Heinemann Bookshop at www.heinemann.co.uk/library to browse our catalogue and order online.

First published in Great Britain by Heinemann Library, Halley Court, Jordan Hill, Oxford OX2 8EJ, part of Harcourt Education.
Heinemann is a registered trademark of Harcourt Education Ltd.

Editorial: Nancy Dickmann and Kate Bellamy
Design: David Poole and Paul Myerscough
Illustrations: Geoff Ward
Picture Research: Rebecca Sodergren
Production: Séverine Ribierre

Originated by Dot Gradations
Printed and bound in China by South China Printing Company

The paper used to print this book comes from sustainable resources.

ISBN 0 431 189668
08 07 06 05 04
10 9 8 7 6 5 4 3 2 1

### British Library Cataloguing in Publication Data

Solway, Andrew
Hidden Life: What's Living in Your Classroom?
  579.1'755
A full catalogue record for this book is available from the British Library.

### Acknowledgements

The publishers would like to thank the following for permission to reproduce photographs:

Alamy p. **10a**; Ardea p. **24** (Steve Hopkins); Corbis p. **17b** (Jacqui Hurst), p. **18a** (Charles Gupton), p. **18b** (George D Lepp); Getty images/photodisk p. **4a**; Martin Sookias p. **14**; Medical-on-line p. **19**; NHPA p. **12** (Michael Leach); Oxford Scientific Films p. **26** (Tony Bomford), p. **27** (Harold Taylor); Science Photo Library pp. **8a**, **8b**; Science Photo Library p. **4b** (Dr Tony Brain and David Parker), p. **5** (Philippe Plailly Eurolios), pp. **6a**, **25** (Dr Jeremy Burgess), p. **6b** (Andrew Syred), pp. **7**, **17a** (Rosenfeld Images Ltd), p. **9** (Sinclair Stammers), p. **10b** (M I Walker), p. **11** (Jan Hinsch), pp. **13**, **22a** (Eye of Science), pp. **15a**, **16** (David Scharf), p. **15b** (Andrew Syred), p. **20** (Linda Steinmark, Custom Medical Stock Photo), pp. **21a**, **23** (A B Dowsett), p. **21b** (Dr Linda Stannard, UCT), p. **22b** (Damien Lovegrove)

Cover photograph of a head louse, reproduced with permission of Science Photo Library.

Every effort has been made to contact copyright holders of any material reproduced in this book. Any omissions will be rectified in subsequent printings if notice is given to the publishers.

# Contents

Any words appearing in the text in bold, **like this,** are explained in the Glossary.

Many of the photos in this book were taken using a microscope. In the captions you may see a number that tells you how much they have been enlarged. For example, a photo marked '(x200)' is about 200 times bigger than in real life.

# Under the microscope

During the school day, a classroom is full of life. But at night and at weekends, there isn't much life – is there? Well, you may have plants in your classroom, or a fish tank or pets, but even if you don't, there is plenty of life around the classroom. You just have to look closely enough.

If you could look at your classroom through a **microscope**, you would see all kinds of living things that are completely invisible to the naked eye – a world of hidden life.

*This photo (x200) shows clumps of bacteria on the point of a pin (at this magnification the point looks flat). It gives some idea of just how tiny bacteria are.*

*This classroom looks empty but there is hidden life everywhere, if you look hard enough.*

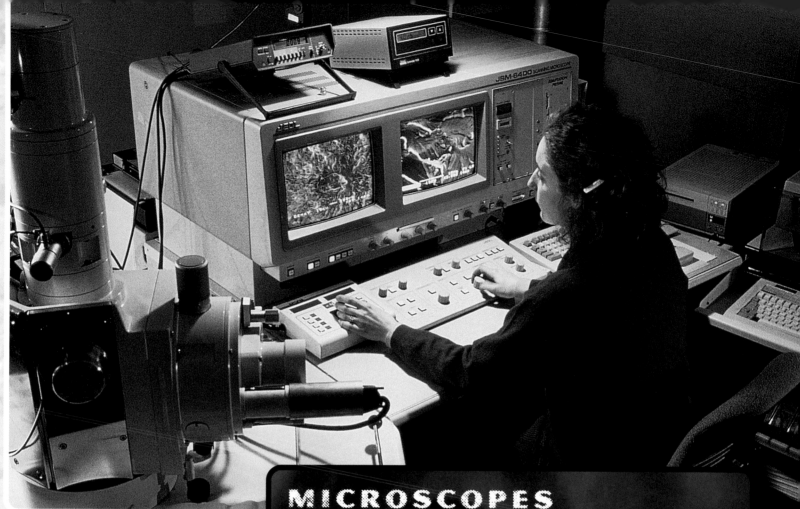

## Getting up close

Even at low magnification, you can find creatures with your microscope. For instance, you might find that a small stain in a damp corner of the room is made up of a mass of tiny threads. It is a **mould fungus**, a relative of mushrooms and toadstools.

## Moving closer

If you zoom in closer, you will start to see microscopic creatures everywhere. The most common of them are

## MICROSCOPES

We know what tiny creatures such as bacteria and viruses look like because scientists have been able to study them using microscopes. The type of microscope you may have used yourself at home or at school (a light microscope) can magnify objects up to about 1800 times. But to look at really tiny things, scientists use **electron microscopes**. This kind of microscope can magnify objects up to half a million times.

**bacteria**. These simple-looking creatures are made up of just a single **cell**. An average-sized bacterium is around a few micrometres (millionths of a metre) long.

## Smallest of all

Increase the magnification of your microscope to its

limits and you might be able to see the smallest creatures of all – **viruses**. Viruses cannot survive without the help of a living cell. They reproduce by getting inside a cell and taking it over. They then use the cell to produce thousands more viruses.

5

# Microbes in muck

You probably have a cloakroom at school where you can leave your coat and shoes. This is good because otherwise you might bring in all sorts of unwelcome visitors!

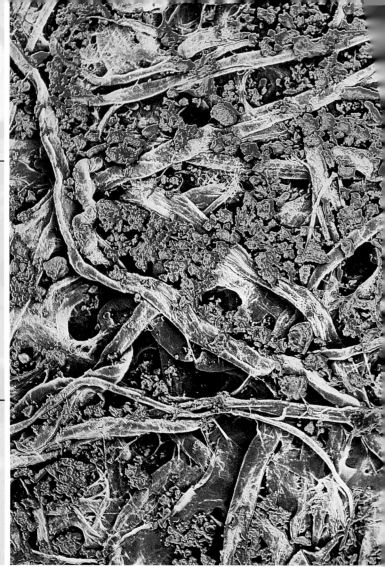

*Soil particles, shown in green on the right, are home to all kinds of bacteria and other microbes. Dung microbes are sometime found in soil, and can include the bacteria Escherichia coli and **fungi** such as Pilobolus (shown below).*

The soles of your shoes have bits of dirt and mud stuck to them. When you arrive at school, you bring this dirt with you. If you live on a farm or in the country, this dirt could include interesting things like animal dung!

## Microbes in mud and dung

Yuck! Mud and dung sound like horrible places for any creature to live. But for **microbes**, mud and dung – especially dung – are rich sources of food.

All kinds of microbes live in dung. They make up almost a third of its weight. The rest of the living world relies on these microbes, because they break down the dung into nutrients that enrich the soil. Without them, we would be surrounded everywhere by piles of dung.

## Treating sewage

Because **bacteria** are so good at digesting dung, we use them to treat **sewage** (the human waste from our towns and cities). Sewage is packed with dung microbes. At a sewage works, waste is diluted with water and pumped into large tanks. Air is then bubbled through the water to help the microbes in it to grow. The microbes convert the sewage into **carbon dioxide** and other harmless chemicals.

## Making you sick

Although dung microbes are useful, it's important that they don't get into the wrong places, because they can make people ill. For instance if *E. coli* bacteria get on to food, they can cause food poisoning.

*Tanks in a sewage treatment works where sewage is digested by microbes.*

## BACTERIA FACTS

You could fit about 1000 average-sized bacteria across a pinhead. They may be round, rod-shaped, comma-shaped or spiral. Most bacteria have a hard outer wall, and sometimes a layer of sticky slime outside that.

Bacteria are wizards at chemistry. They can use all sorts of unpromising materials as food – some bacteria eat rubber, and others eat petrol!

# feeling lousy

If you have an itchy head that won't stop itching, you might have tiny guests in your hair. Head lice are small, flattened insects that hide in people's hair and feed on their blood. Anyone can get head lice, especially in the busy working conditions of a classroom.

## Parasitic passengers

Head lice are **parasites** – they live on humans (their **hosts**) and get all their nourishment from human blood. Lice cannot fly or jump. They move from host to host by simply walking from one person's head to another.

A head louse (x160). You can see the strong claws it uses for holding on to its host, its **antennae**, and the **sensory hairs** all over its body.

Special extra-fine combs can be used to check for head lice and nits. Nits are usually easier to notice. They look a bit like dandruff but can not be brushed off easily.

In a busy, crowded place like a school this can easily happen, so once lice get into one person's hair, they often get spread around.

## Hard to spot

Head lice are well-adapted to their parasitic life style. They are tiny – little bigger than a pinhead – and dull brown in colour, which makes them hard to spot in hair. Their bodies are flattened and they have strong claws for holding on to hairs.

Lice have no eyes, because in the thick forest of a person's hair, sight is not very useful. They rely instead on their senses of smell and touch to find their way around. They feed by biting a tiny hole in the scalp and sucking out blood.

Head lice take only about three weeks to grow from eggs to adults, so they can increase in numbers very quickly. However, they live for only about 30 days.

Female lice stick their egg cases ('nits') to hairs, very close to the scalp. When they hatch, the young lice look like small adults. They take about a week to grow to full size.

## Getting rid of lice

Normal shampoo or combing can not get rid of lice. You need a special shampoo to get rid of adult lice. Nits are harder to dislodge. Regular combing with an extra-fine comb (a nit comb) is the best way to remove them.

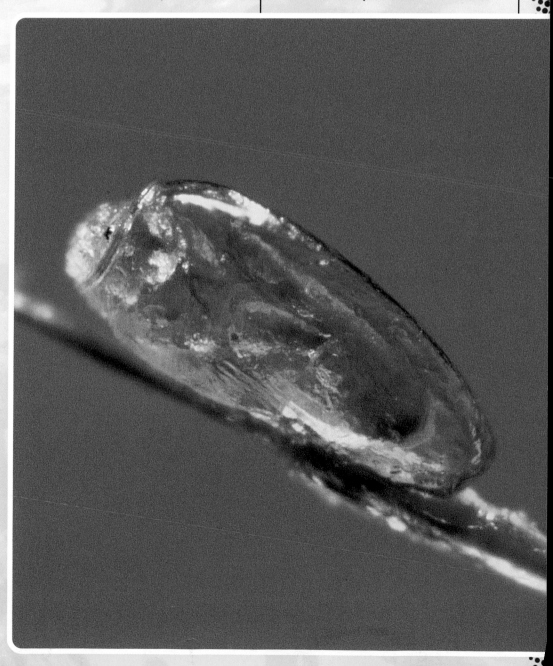

*A louse egg case (nit) with a developing louse inside. At this stage the egg case is almost transparent, which makes it very difficult to see.*

# Micro-plants

Some classrooms have an aquarium. It's fun to watch the fish, and they are easy to look after. But occasionally the water goes all green and scummy, or a green film forms on the glass. These problems are caused by microscopic, plant-like creatures called **algae**.

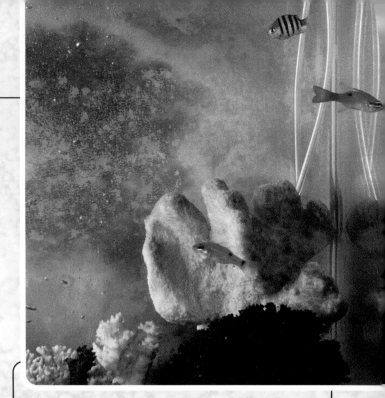

🔵 Fish are not the only living things in an aquarium.

⚓ Most algae like Spirogyra reproduce by simply dividing in two. But sometimes two filaments will join up, as here (x1000). Once this has happened the algae form thick-walled spores, which can survive cold and drying out.

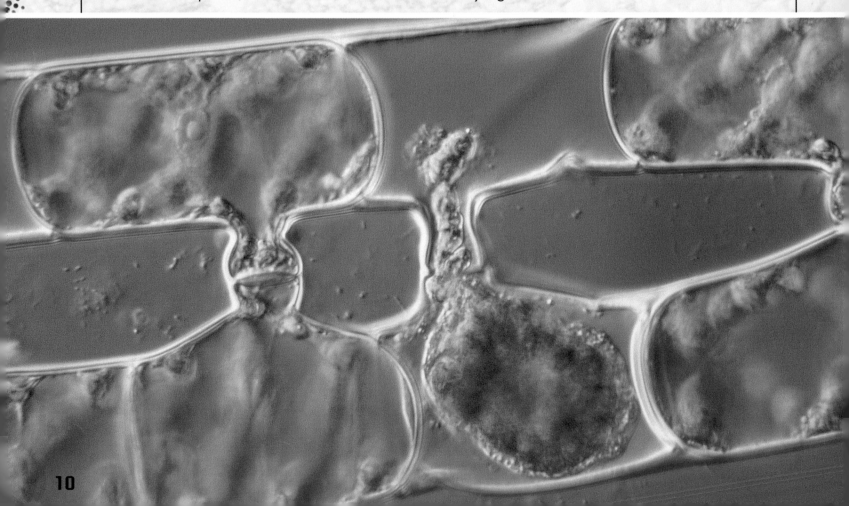

## Sun-worshippers

Like plants, green algae need sunlight to survive. This is because they do not eat food, but make it from water, sunlight and **carbon dioxide**.

Plants and algae are green because they contain a pigment (coloured chemical) called **chlorophyll**. The chlorophyll is a key part of the process for making food using sunlight energy. Just like plant cells, algae contain **chloroplasts**, where sunlight energy is turned into sugary food.

## Spirals and star filaments

Green algae are microscopic, but some of them join together to make long strings, or filaments. One of the best known of these algae is *Spirogyra*. They get their name from the fact that they have a long, spiral chloroplast. A related group of algae, called *Zygnema*, have star-shaped chloroplasts.

## LIVE-IN BACTERIA

Some bacteria can make food from sunlight, just like plants and green algae. They are called **cyanobacteria**. Scientists think that millions of years ago, close relatives of the cyanobacteria began to live inside the cells of larger creatures. These 'live-in' cyanobacteria became the chloroplasts that we see in plants and algae.

## Skeletons of glass

Not all green algae are green — some are brown! Brown stains that sometimes form on the glass of an aquarium are caused by algae called **diatoms**. Diatoms do contain chlorophyll, but they also have other pigments that make them look brown.

Under the microscope, diatoms are tiny jewels. Each kind of diatom has its own particular, beautifully shaped, glassy outer shell. The shell surface is covered in fine lines. These lines are rows of ultra-tiny holes, which allow the cell inside to keep in touch with the outside world.

*Freshwater diatoms (x240) come in a variety of shapes and sizes.*

# Ear mites

Many classes have pet mice to look after instead of fish. Mice can have problems with **parasites** called ear mites. Ear mites are smaller than head lice, but they are nastier. Luckily, they don't live on humans.

Mites are not insects, but close relatives of spiders, so they have eight legs rather than six. Ear mites can affect mice, dogs, cats, rabbits and other pets, and a related kind of mite causes the skin disease mange in pets and some wild animals.

*The irritation that ear mites cause makes the host animal, in this case a mouse, scratch itself and tear the skin.*

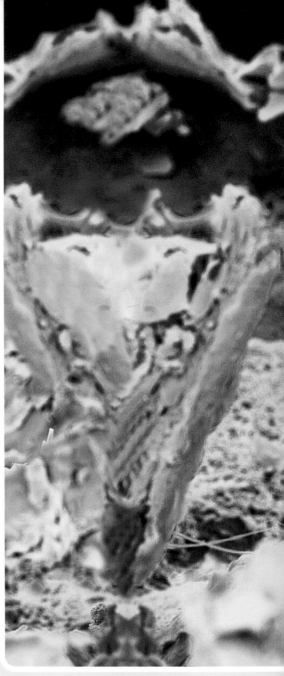

## 'Mitey' lives

Ear mites are hard to see, but microscopes show they have short legs and round bodies. When ear mites hatch, the **larvae** only have six legs. They feed on earwax and skin oils in the **host**'s ear canal. After a week the larvae **moult** and become **protonymphs**. They then feed for 3 to 5 days

An itch mite (x425) on the skin surface. Female itch mites are about 0.4 to 0.5 mm long, while males are smaller (about 0.3 mm).

## Ill effects

When ear mites first get into an animal, the host feels no ill effects. But as mite numbers rise, their droppings and the poisons they produce irritate the insides of the ears. The ears become sore and itchy, and produce too much wax. Scratching causes the ears to bleed. Under a microscope, the dried blood from infected ears is crawling with mites.

and moult again to become **deutonymphs**. Deutonymphs are very strange creatures. Although they are not yet adults, they mate with male mites. Even more strange is that it is not clear at this stage what sex they will be as adults. After mating the deutonymph moults again and becomes either a male or female adult.

## A 'MITEY' BIG NUISANCE!

Mites and their larger relatives, ticks, cause all sorts of headaches for people. Some kinds are parasites on people or farm animals and pets. Others are plant pests, damaging food crops. But mites are not all bad. Mites that live in the soil are important in keeping the soil fertile, and some **predatory** mites eat plant pests.

# Billions of bacteria

One of the main sources of hidden life in the classroom is you and your classmates. All of us carry **bacteria** around with us on our skin. Each person has about 1000 billion skin bacteria – that's over 160 times more bacteria than there are people in the world!

Skin bacteria prefer moist, warm places, and they need a source of food – usually sweat or skin oils. So there are more bacteria in warm, damp places, like the armpits, than on other parts of the skin.

Even though there can be lots of bacteria around the sink, washing your hands regularly is one of the best ways to avoid harmful germs.

## Helpful bacteria

Skin bacteria don't usually do us any harm – in fact they help protect us from disease-causing bacteria. This is because it is hard for disease bacteria to survive and grow on the skin in competition with the bacteria that already live there.

Although our normal bacteria are not harmful, we do pick up 'foreign' bacteria from other people and from things we touch. Some of these can cause disease, particularly if they get into the mouth or if we have a cut. This is why it is important to wash your hands before eating and to clean cuts.

## Washing your hands

The areas around a sink are usually damp, and towels get damp regularly. Bacteria can grow in these areas, especially if towels are not changed frequently. Even bars of soap can have bacteria living on them, if they are used a lot and are often wet.

Despite this, washing your hands thoroughly with ordinary soap will get rid of nearly all the germs on them – even if the soap does have bacteria on it. But it is important to dry your hands well, because bacteria can survive much better on wet hands.

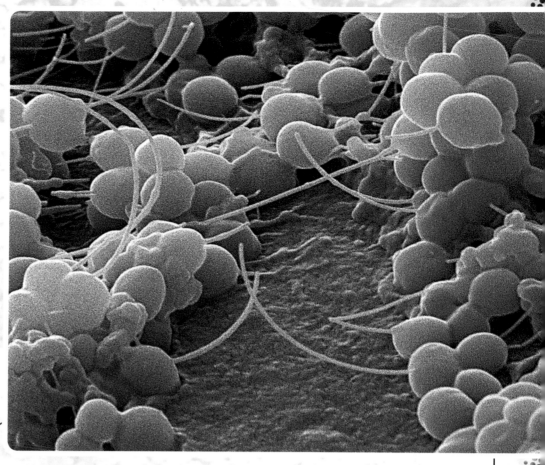

*The bacteria* Staphylococcus epidermidis *(x17,700) are commonly found on human skin.*

*A close up of skin (x2000) showing dead cells flaking away from the surface.*

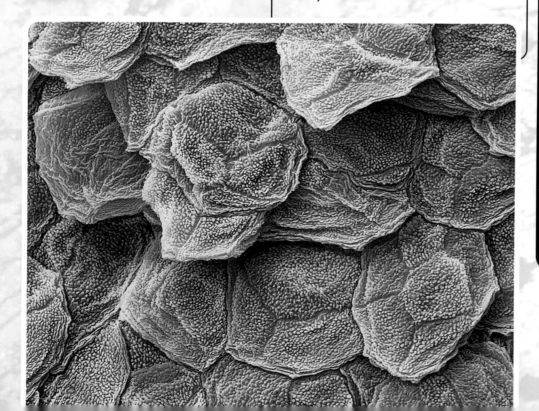

## BACTERIAL DEFENCES

The outer part of the skin is made up of about 15 layers of dead cells, cemented together with fats and oils. This is a tough barrier for bacteria to get through. Flakes of skin are continually being worn away, but they are replaced by new skin **cells**.

# Microbe-packed food

Do you take a packed lunch to school? If you do, it might include cheese sandwiches and a yoghurt. Both these foods are full of **microbes**.

For thousands of years people have been making bread, yoghurt and cheese. All these foods are made using microbes.

## Bread

Without the help of microbes, bread would be flat and hard. To make it light and airy, you need to add yeast. Yeast is a microscopic creature – not a **bacterium**, but a type of **fungus**. The yeast feeds on the sugars in bread dough, and produces **carbon dioxide** as a waste product. The carbon dioxide gets caught as tiny bubbles within the dough. These bubbles of carbon dioxide are what make the bread rise.

*Unlike other types of fungi, yeasts are single cells (x400), rather than tiny threads.*

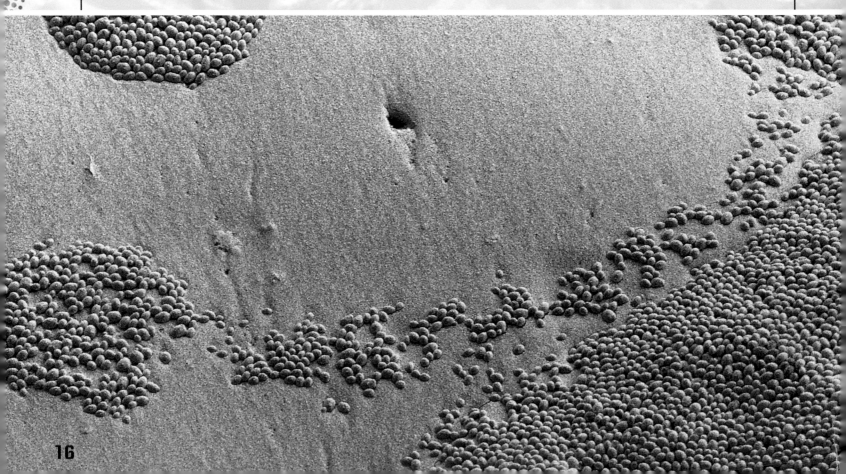

## Yoghurt

When you eat bread, the microbes are already dead (baking kills off the yeast). But when you eat yoghurt, the microbes are still alive (if it is 'live' yoghurt).

Yoghurt is milk that is full of bacteria. But not just any bacteria – a very specific kind, called *Lactobacillus*. Like the yeast in bread, the *Lactobacillus* feeds on sugars in the milk. But unlike the yeast, it produces acid as a waste product. This acid is what gives the yoghurt its sharp taste.

## CHEESE FACTS

Four litres of milk (about three kilos in weight) yields less than half a kilo of cheese. The weight that is lost is all the water in milk.

*These raw cheeses depend on bacteria in order to ripen.*

## Cheese

Cheese is similar to yoghurt in that it is made from milk and acid-producing bacteria. But cheese-makers add another ingredient – **rennet** – which, along with the acid, makes the milk separate into milk solids (curds) and a watery liquid (whey). The whey is drained off, then the curds are pressed – lightly at first, then with a pressure of several tonnes. The cheese is now left for a few months to ripen in a cool place. During this time bacteria continue to grow slowly and make further changes to the cheese, which improve its flavour.

*Some cheeses contain fungi as well as bacteria! The veins in blue cheeses such as Stilton are produced by a **mould fungus**.*

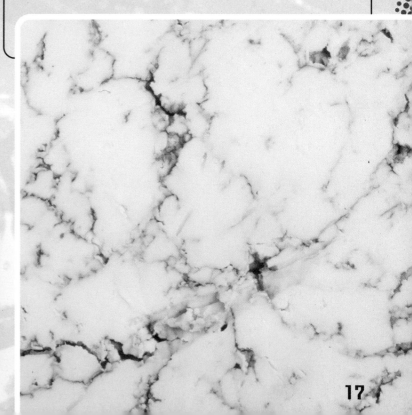

# Chocolate microbes?

Maybe you have chocolate or sweets with your packed lunch. There aren't any **microbes** in these foods, but microbes were essential for making them.

## Making chocolate

Chocolate is made from cacao beans — the seeds of the cacao tree. When they are growing, the beans are encased in a large pod. To make chocolate, workers harvest the ripe red or yellow pods, split them and take out the beans. Then they

*Microbes have probably been used to make the food you and your classmates eat for lunch.*

pile up the beans, cover them with banana leaves and leave them to **ferment**. After this they are dried and roasted.

*A ripe cacao pod split open to show the beans within.*

The fermenting process takes away some of the bitterness of the cacao beans and develops their rich chocolatey flavour. Without this process, chocolate just wouldn't taste the same!

Fermentation relies on naturally occurring **bacteria** and yeasts, which feed on sugars in the beans. Air has to be kept out for fermentation to take place, which is why the beans are piled together and covered.

## Gummy sweets

Gums, pastilles and jellies all contain a sweet, gummy substance called **xanthan**. (pronounced 'zan-than'). This is made by bacteria called *Xanthomonas campestris*. Xanthan can be used to thicken water into a gel. Besides sweets it is

*A colony of Xanthomonas campestris bacteria. The bacteria themselves are yellow, but the xanthan gum they produce is colourless.*

used to make ice cream, salad dressings and some paints. *Xanthomonas* makes this gummy slime to stop itself from drying out.

### AMAZING HONEY

Sweets are full of sugar, so they should be good places for microbes to grow. But in fact microbes don't grow well in concentrated sugar. Honey is one substance that microbes really cannot live in. If it is kept in a sealed container it will last for years without spoiling.

# Colds and flu

If you go to school with a cold, be careful to use a hanky if you cough or sneeze. Otherwise, you will spread a cloud of germs around the classroom. The germs that cause colds and flu are not **bacteria**. They are even smaller things called **viruses**.

The viruses that cause colds and flu spread from person to person on tiny droplets of liquid, which fly into the air when an infected person coughs or sneezes. When someone else breathes in some of these droplets, they become infected. Luckily the body's defences can usually cope with the infection, and we soon get better.

## How do viruses work?

Viruses are unbelievably tiny packages of chemicals. They cannot grow or reproduce unless they can get inside the **cells** of another living thing. Viruses are very simple structures. The outside is a protective **protein** 'coat', inside which are the virus's **genes** – the complex chemicals that make it possible for the virus to reproduce.

This photograph has caught the cloud of droplets that shoot out of the nose and mouth when we sneeze. If the person is infected with cold or flu viruses, many of these droplets will be carrying viruses.

When a virus gets into a cell, the virus's genes join themselves on to the cell's genes. The genes contain the instructions for making the virus take over from the cell's normal instructions, and the cell becomes a virus-making factory.

Thousands of copies of the virus are made, and eventually the cell bursts, releasing the viruses to infect other cells.

## Other viruses

Viruses cause many other diseases besides colds and flu. Mumps, sore throats and the brain disease meningitis are just some of the other disease they cause in humans. And viruses infect just about all other types of living thing too — even bacteria.

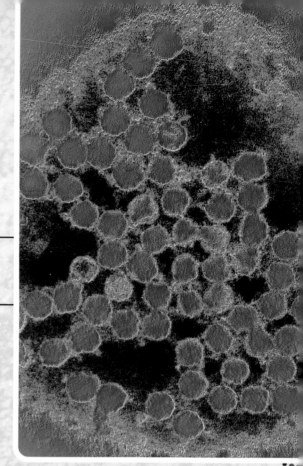

*This photo shows a cluster of cold viruses (about x200,000).*

## NO METABOLISM

A living cell is like a chemical factory. One set of chemicals (the cell's food) are broken down to produce energy. This energy is then used to make other chemicals — the proteins and other substances that make up the cell. The sum total of this chemical activity is called the cell's **metabolism**.

Viruses have no metabolism. Instead, they take over the metabolism of a living cell.

*These green blobs are influenza viruses (viruses that cause flu). They are seven or eight times bigger than the cold viruses shown above.*

# Allergy alert

On hot summer days, your classroom windows are probably wide open. Some people might begin to sneeze and snuffle, but it's not because they have colds. **Pollen** grains and **spores** in the air are causing hay fever.

Hay fever is an allergy – an illness caused by the body over-reacting to harmless substances. In hay fever, pollen grains or spores get into the nose and cause it to produce lots of mucus, as if we have a cold or flu.

*Pollen grains of the hollyhock, Althaea rosea (x850). Pollen grains from different plants can look very different. Many have beautiful, sculpted shapes.*

*Pollen causes hay fever sufferers to sneeze.*

## Pollen

Pollen is not a living thing, but it carries life hidden inside it. It is a very fine, yellow dust produced by flowering plants. Pollen grains are the male sex cells of plants, encased in a tough protective coat. If pollen lands on a flower of the same kind of plant, it joins up with egg cells in the flower to make seeds.

## Dust from fungi

Pollen is not the only kind of 'living dust'. Damp areas of plaster on walls or ceilings are places where **moulds** can grow. A mould is a kind of **fungus**, and fungi reproduce by releasing clouds of tiny **spores**. Like pollen, these spores can cause allergies.

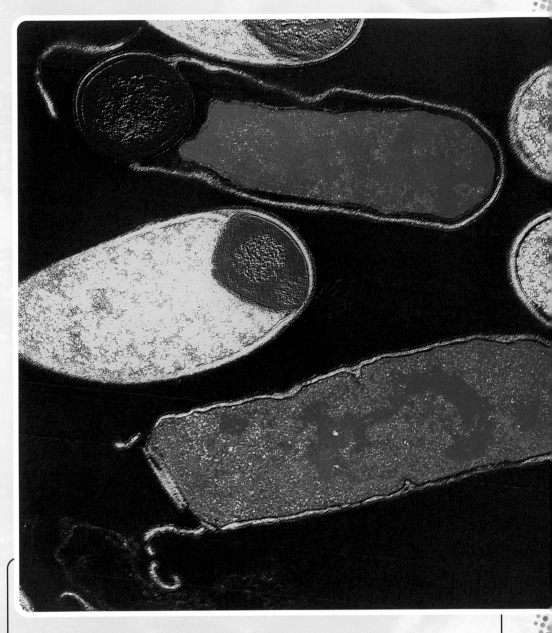

The oval shapes inside some of these bacteria are developing spores.

## Bacterial mummies

Some kinds of **bacteria** can also make spores, but these are not the same as fungal spores. A bacterial spore is a sort of 'mummified bacterium' – except that the bacterium inside is not dead. There is no food and little moisture in the air.

Without protection, most bacteria would quickly die. So a spore-forming bacterium protects its **genes**! It makes a copy of the genes, then builds up a series of protective coatings around them. The result is a spore.

Inside their protective spore, the genes can survive drying out, high temperatures and even radiation. When water and food become available again, the bacterium 'comes to life'.

# Chewing up old books

Old textbooks or classwork can be left untouched in store cupboards for months. They make a perfect home for booklice. Booklice are almost microscopic, transparent insects that live in books and papers. Booklice are not true lice, although they are quite closely related. Booklice are also distantly related to **aphids** (greenfly). They look quite similar to aphids.

> *Booklice have chewing mouthparts, designed to scrape food from a surface and grind it up.*

# PARTHENOGENESIS

When a female animal or plant's eggs develop without needing a male to **fertilize** them, it is called **parthenogenesis**.

Aphids also reproduce this way. During the summer months, all aphids that are born are wingless females. These aphids can lay eggs without the need for fertilisation. But eggs that hatch as autumn approaches produce winged male and female aphids. The males and females mate, and the female lays her eggs before the winter comes. The eggs lay dormant over winter, then hatch the next spring.

## Harmless guests

Booklice are tiny, whitish, wingless insects that are hard to spot without a torch and a magnifying glass. Booklice do not bite or cause disease, so small numbers of them can live in a building completely unnoticed. However, large numbers can cause damage to books, furnishings and wallpaper.

Booklice eat **cereals**, pollen, fragments of dead insects and the starchy paste that is used in book binding. But their favourite foods are mould and **mildew**. They like warmth and damp, and they avoid bright light. A pile of mouldy old books in a warm, damp cupboard is a booklouse's idea of heaven!

## All girls

Booklice are nearly all female: males are very rare. Booklice eggs develop without being **fertilized** by a male. Each female lays about 60 eggs. She puts the eggs near a source of food, so that when the young **nymphs** hatch, their first meal is all ready for them to eat.

Aphids, like booklice, are unusual because they can lay eggs and can give birth to live young. Not many animals can do both.

# Silverfish and firebrats

In a damp spot near the classroom sink you might find some other hidden residents. Silverfish are over 1 centimetre long, but you are unlikely to see them. They hide during the day, and come out at night to feed.

## Silverfish

Silverfish are flat, elongated insects. They get their name from the shiny, silvery-grey scales that cover their bodies. They have two **antennae** on their head and three long, thin bristles on their tails (silverfish and their relatives are sometimes called 'bristletails').

Silverfish like to live in cool, damp places such as around sinks and baths or in damp basements. During the day silverfish hide, but at night they come out looking for water and food.

*A silverfish on paper. Insects always have three parts to their bodies – the head, the* **thorax** *(middle) and the* **abdomen** *(back part). In silverfish each of these body parts is divided into several segments.*

*Firebrats are not often seen, because they usually stick to dark places and they can move very quickly.*

Like booklice, silverfish enjoy book bindings and paste. But they eat a much wider range of food than booklice, including glue, wallpaper paste, photographs, fabrics, **cereals** and leather.

Many insects live only a few weeks or months, but silverfish can live for 2 or more years. Female silverfish lay over 100 eggs during a lifetime. The young that hatch out look like small adults, except that they are white rather than silvery grey.

Both silverfish and firebrats are tough customers. They can survive for many months without food.

## Firebrats

Firebrats look similar to silverfish, except that they are mottled grey rather than silvery. The two are closely related, but

firebrats like warm, dry places rather than damp ones. They could live in the school boiler room, or in the insulation around central heating pipes.

## THE EARLIEST INSECTS?

Many types of insects have lost their wings over time. The ancestors of booklice were winged, but over thousands of years they lost their wings because wings were of no use in the **environment** that they lived in.

But silverfish are different – their ancestors never had wings. They are **primitive** insects, which means that they are like the very earliest types of insect.

# Table of sizes

Although all hidden life is tiny, there is a huge range of sizes. To a flea, a grain of pollen seems just as tiny as the flea seems to us!

These organisms are 20 times bigger than normal.

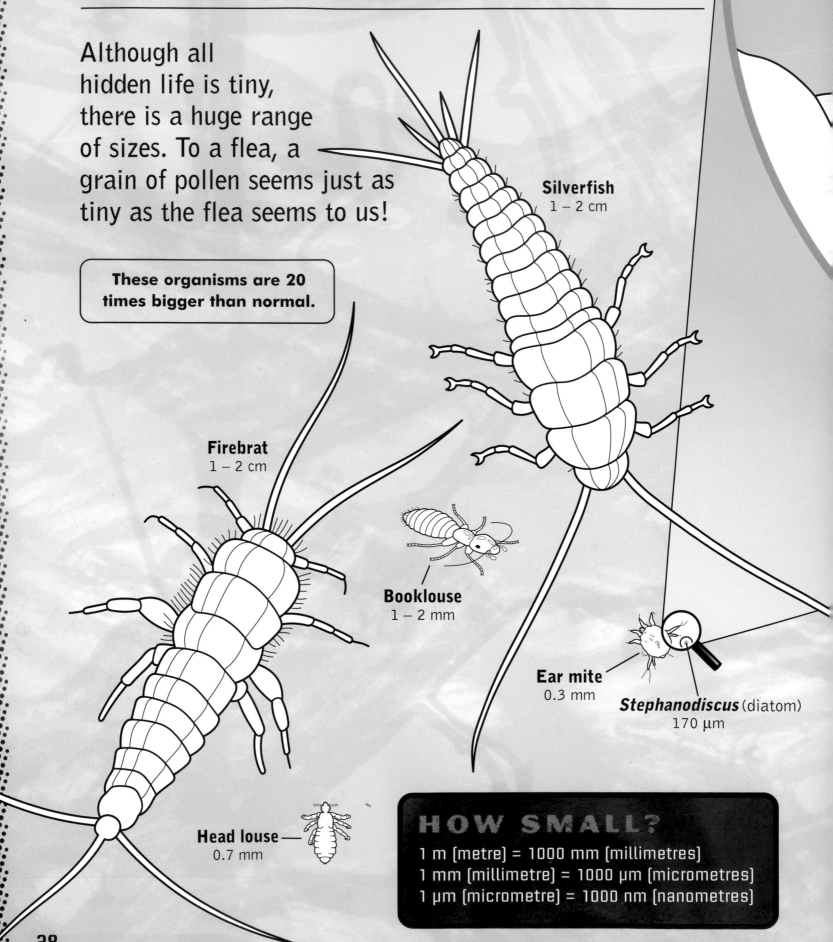

**Silverfish**
1 – 2 cm

**Firebrat**
1 – 2 cm

**Booklouse**
1 – 2 mm

**Ear mite**
0.3 mm

*Stephanodiscus* (diatom)
170 µm

**Head louse** —
0.7 mm

## HOW SMALL?

1 m [metre] = 1000 mm [millimetres]
1 mm [millimetre] = 1000 µm [micrometres]
1 µm [micrometre] = 1000 nm [nanometres]

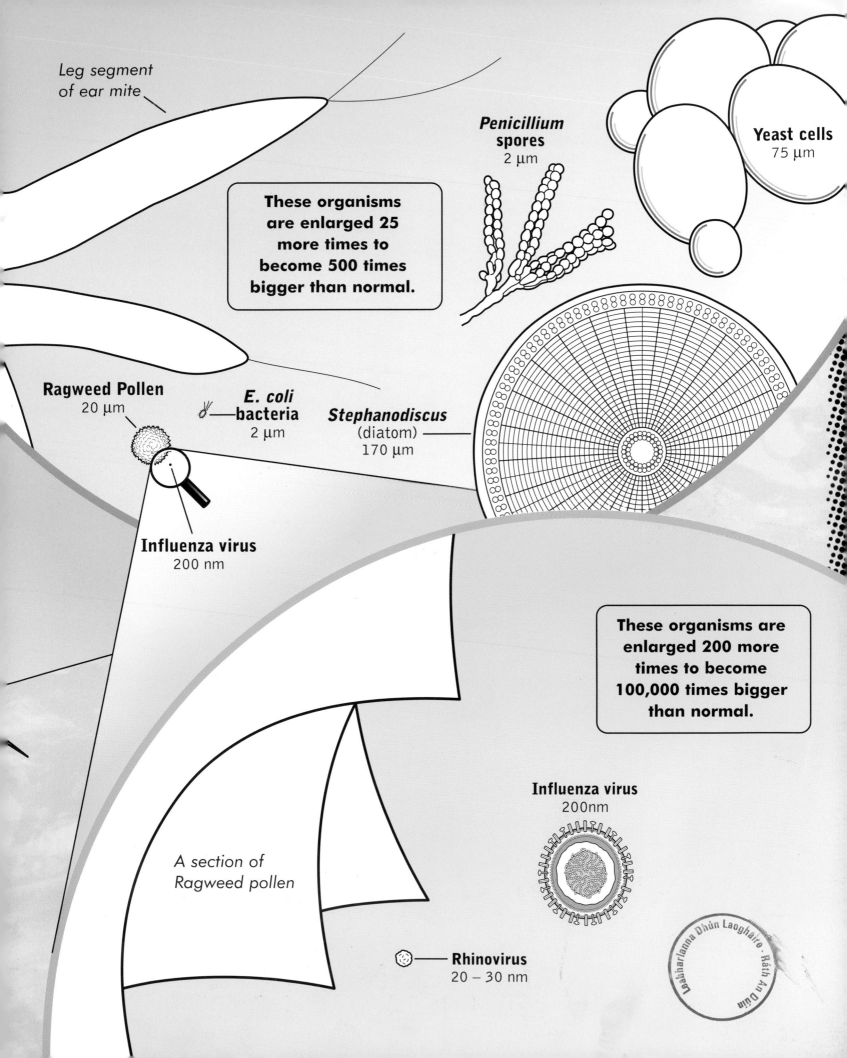

Leg segment
of ear mite

***Penicillium*
spores**
2 μm

**Yeast cells**
75 μm

**These organisms
are enlarged 25
more times to
become 500 times
bigger than normal.**

**Ragweed Pollen**
20 μm

***E. coli*
bacteria**
2 μm

***Stephanodiscus***
(diatom)
170 μm

**Influenza virus**
200 nm

**These organisms are
enlarged 200 more
times to become
100,000 times bigger
than normal.**

**Influenza virus**
200nm

*A section of
Ragweed pollen*

**Rhinovirus**
20 – 30 nm

# Glossary

**abdomen** back section of an insect, which contains most of the body organs

**algae** large group of plant-like creatures, most of which are microscopic

**allergic reaction** when the body overreacts to something that you breathe in or eat or get on your skin. It can cause sneezing, or a rash or sickness.

**antennae** the two feelers on an insect's head

**aphid** small insect that lives on plants and sucks their sap

**bacterium** very tiny creature with only a single cell. Bacteria are different from other single-celled creatures because their DNA is not in a nucleus.

**carbon dioxide** gas that is found in small amounts in the air

**cell** building block of living things. Some living things are single cells, others are made up of billions of cells working together.

**cereal** wheat, barley, oats and similar food crops

**chlorophyll** green pigment (coloured chemical) found in plants that traps light energy from the sun. The plants use the energy to make food.

**chloroplast** tiny part within plant cells that turns light energy into food

**cyanobacterium** type of bacterium that can make their own food from light, water and carbon dioxide, like plants can

**deutonymph** third stage in the growth of some mites. Deutonymphs can mate but are not fully developed adults.

**diatom** type of algae found in fresh or seawater that has a skeleton made of a substance called silica

**electron microscope** very powerful microscope that can magnify objects up to half a million times

**environment** place where a living thing lives, and the other creatures that live there

**ferment** when food ferments, microbes turn the sugar in it into something else, like an acid or alcohol

**fertilization** when a male sex cell joins with the egg cell of a female to form a new life

**fungus** group of living plant-like things, including mushrooms, moulds and yeasts

**genes** contain information that enables a cell to build itself, get energy, grow and reproduce

**host** the animal or plant that a parasite lives on

**larva** young stage of some types of creature. Larvae look different from adults, and may have to go through a changing stage in order to become adults.

**metabolism** all the chemical activity that goes on inside a living cell, or collection of cells

**microbe** microscopic creature such as bacteria, algae and viruses

**microscope** instrument for magnifying tiny objects

**mildew** fungus that infects plants and shows as a powdery covering on affected parts of the plant

**mould** type of fungus that can grow on or in a wide range of substances, from damp plaster to cheese

**moult** to shed hair, feathers or skin

**nymph** the young stage of some types of creature. Nymphs usually look similar to their parents, and change gradually into adults over several moults.

**parasite** creature that lives on or in another living creature and takes food from it, without giving any benefit in return

**parthenogenesis** form of reproduction in which eggs develop into young without being fertilized

**pollen** fine powder produced by flowers to fertilize other flowers

**predator** animal that hunts and kills another animal for food

**primitive** ancient or early state of something. A primitive creature is one that is like its early ancestors.

**protein** important group of living substances that are used to build structures within living things, and to control the thousands of chemical reactions that happen inside cells

**protonymph** second stage in the growth of some mites

**rennet** material made from the stomachs of young calves that is used to curdle milk in cheese-making

**sensory hair** hair on the body of a creature that is sensitive to touch or vibrations

**sewage** watery wastes from the toilets and drains of houses and from factories

**spores**   fungal spores are like very tiny fungal 'seeds'. Bacterial spores are bacteria that have formed a tough outer coat to help them survive difficult conditions.

**thorax**   middle section of an insect's body that the legs, and wings, if it has them, are attached to

**virus**   very tiny microbe that has to infect a living cell in order to grow or reproduce

**xanthan**   a gummy substance formed by certain types of bacteria

# further reading

*Awesome Bugs: Spiders and Scorpions*, Anna Claybourne (Franklin Watts, 2003)

*Cells and Life: The Diversity of Life*, Robert Snedden (Heinemann Library, 2002)

*Cells and Life: The World of the Cell*, Robert Snedden (Heinemann Library, 2002)

*Horrible Science: Microscopic Monsters*, Nick Arnold, illustrated by Tony de Saulles (Barbour Books, 2001)

*The Illustrated Wildlife Encyclopedia: Bugs & Minibeasts*, John Farndon, Jen Green and Barbara Taylor (Southwater Press, 2002)

*Microlife: A World of Microorganisms*, Robert Snedden (Heinemann Library, 2000)

# Websites

**Cells Alive! (www.cellsalive.com)**
Pictures, videos and interactive pages about cells and microbes. The How Big? page shows the sizes of creatures from mites to viruses.

**Virtual Microscopy (www.micro.magnet.fsu.edu/primer/virtual/virtual.html)**
On this interactive website you can pick from a selection of samples, adjust the focus, change the magnification, and use a whole range of powerful microscopes.

**Microbe Zoo (www.commtechlab.msu.edu/sites/dlc-me/zoo/)**
A site about strange creatures from the world of microbes.

# Index

# Titles in the *Hidden Life* series include:

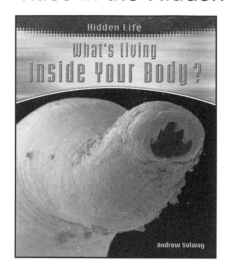

Hardback      0 431 18962 5

Hardback      0 431 18965 X

Hardback      0 431 18964 1

Hardback      0 431 18963 3

Hardback      0 431 18966 8

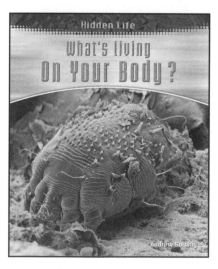

Hardback      0 431 18961 7

Find out about the other titles in this series on our website www.heinemann.co.uk/library